RUGBY FROM BEGINNERS TO PRO

Ultimate Guide to Rules, Strategies, Techniques, Skill Development, Drills, Positions, Team Dynamics, Fitness Training, Scrum and Lineout Tactics

BEN G. ELSTON

COPYRIGHT © 2023 BY BEN G. ELSTON

All rights reserved. No part of this publication may be reproduced, distributed, or transmitted in any form or by any means, including photocopying, recording, or other electronic or mechanical methods, without the prior written permission of the publisher, except in the case of brief quotations embodied in critical reviews and certain other noncommercial uses permitted by copyright law.

CHAPTER ONE 5
  INTRODUCTION TO RUGBY 5
    Basic Rules and Gameplay 11
CHAPTER TWO 15
  RUGBY FUNDAMENTALS AND GEAR .. 15
    RUGBY BALL AND SAFETY
    EQUIPMENT 22
    Replacements and Switches 27
CHAPTER THREE 30
  PASSING AND HANDLING SKILLS IN
  RUGBY 30
    Accuracy and Proper Passing Form 33
    Fending and Offloading 35
    Chasing Low and High Balls 36
    Evasive Running and Directional
    Changing 38
CHAPTER FOUR 41

RUGBY TACKLES AND DEFENSE 41

Lineouts and Mauls: Defensive Techniques......................................46

CHAPTER FIVE 51

KICKING AND GAME MANAGEMENT IN RUGBY..51

CHAPTER SIX...61

RUGBY TEAM TACTICS AND PLAYBOOKS 61

Attacking Movements and Patterns 64

Finding Defensive Loopholes 65

Changing Game Situations Adaptation 68

CONCLUSION 72

THANK YOU......................................78

CHAPTER ONE
INTRODUCTION TO RUGBY

Rugby is a physically taxing and captivating sport with a rich history and numerous versions to suit various tastes and playing philosophies. This review of rugby's fundamental rules and gameplay dives into the sport's history and numerous variations, such as Rugby Union, Rugby League, and Rugby Sevens.

Rugby's beginnings can be found in England in the early 19th century. According to legend, the sport began when a pupil by the name of William Webb Ellis at Rugby School in Warwickshire, England, scooped up the ball and ran with it during a game of football (what Americans refer to as soccer). This impromptu action set the groundwork for a brand-new sport that merged aspects of traditional ball sports with football. Due to this incident, the oval-shaped ball was created and the basic idea that players could carry the ball and run while holding it was established.

As the game gained popularity among different colleges and high schools, each created its own set of regulations. The Rugby Football Union (RFU), which was founded in 1871 by 21 clubs, set the first set of standardized rules. Over time, as the rules were progressively improved, Rugby Union developed its unique qualities. As the sport spread to other nations, international competitions began. Rugby's position on the international stage was further cemented by the Rugby World Cup, which was first held in 1987.

Rugby variants: Union, League, and Sevens

Rugby Union: Rugby Union, sometimes known as "rugby," is the most well-known variety of rugby. Each side consists of 15 men, and the game is characterized by scrums, lineouts, mauls, and rucks as well as a combination of offensive and defensive tactics. To score points, the goal is to carry or kick the ball across the goal line of the opposition. In rugby union, collaboration, dexterous handling, and tactical awareness are highly valued.

Rugby League: Disagreements about pay for missing work in Rugby Union led to the development of Rugby League as a different variation in the late 19th century. It has two teams with 13 players each, two sets of rules, and slightly distinct gameplay dynamics. Compared to Rugby

Union, Rugby League emphasizes pace and open play more so than set pieces. It is famous for its six-tackle rule, which stipulates that after six tackles, the attacking team either kick the ball or turn the ball over to the opposition team.

Rugby Sevens: A quicker-paced variation, rugby sevens has been more popular in recent years, especially after it was included to the Olympic Games in 2016. Matches are played on a smaller pitch with seven players per team. A more open and high-scoring game is the result of the fewer players and shorter halves. Rugby Sevens is an exciting spectator sport because it displays players' speed, agility, and quick thinking.

Basic Rules and Gameplay

The purpose of rugby union and rugby league is to score points by touching down on the opponent's goal line (a "try") or kicking the ball through the goal posts (a "conversion" or "penalty goal"), respectively. A "conversion" or "penalty goal" is worth two points, whereas a "try" is worth five points. At the conclusion of the game, the team with the most points wins.

Running, passing, and kicking the ball are all used in the game. In order to gain territory, players might kick the ball or pass it backward to teammates. Players can tackle opponents to halt their progress, which is one of rugby's distinctive features. Grabbing the ball carrier and bringing them to the ground is a tackle. The player must surrender the ball right away after being tackled so that both teams can compete for possession.

Both Rugby Union and Rugby League depend heavily on set pieces like scrums, lineouts, mauls, and rucks. In a scrum, the two forward packs wrestle for control of the ball by pushing against one another. When the ball crosses the line of play, a lineout occurs where players pull a teammate to grab the ball that is thrown in from the sideline. Players band together to secure possession and generate opportunities for their team during mauls and rucks.

As a whole, rugby is a complex sport with a fascinating past that extends back to the 19th century. Rugby's variants, such as Rugby Union, Rugby League, and Rugby Sevens, are designed to accommodate various playing preferences. Carrying, passing, and kicking the ball are part of the sport's core regulations, which also place a strong emphasis on collaboration, strategy, and physicality. Rugby continues to captivate fans and players worldwide, whether it is played on a large international stage or in tiny communities.

CHAPTER TWO

RUGBY FUNDAMENTALS AND GEAR

Rugby, a team sport that blends physicality, strategy, and cooperation, necessitates a thorough comprehension of its core concepts. The fundamentals of rugby are thoroughly examined in this part, including player positions and duties, field size, equipment including the rugby ball and protective gear, the try, conversion, and penalty scoring systems, as well as the subtleties of substitutions and interchanges.

Comprehending Roles and Positions

Backs and forwards are the two main divisions in rugby positions. Every occupation has particular duties, requirements for talents, and physical demands.

Forwards: Players who are often bigger and stronger make up the front pack. They generally participate in the game's more active phases, like scrummaging, lineouts, and rucks. Important positions in the front pack include:

Props: In the scrum, these players offer strength and stability. Props come in two varieties: loosehead and tighthead.

Hooker: The hooker's primary responsibility is to accurately toss the ball during lineouts and participate in the scrum.

Locks: Also referred to as second-row forwards, locks are critical for supplying force in scrums and for springing to collect the thrown ball in lineouts.

Flankers: These athletes contribute significantly to turnovers during rucks and mauls due to their speed and agility.

Number 8: The number 8 is positioned at the back of the scrum and is responsible for both ball management and acting as a bridge between the forwards and backs.

Backs: The backs typically possess greater agility and ball-handling expertise. They are essential to attacking and producing scoring opportunities. Important positions on the backline consist of:

Halfbacks: The scrum-half and fly-half are included here. The scrum-half coordinates plays and passes the ball from the center of the scrum. The team's assault is led by the fly-half, also known as the playmaker, who also makes crucial decisions and kicks for territory.

Centers: Located in the midst of the defense, centers take part in both offensive and defensive plays. They want to make opportunities and space for their teammates.

Wings: The team's fastest players, the wingers are in charge of completing tries by touching the ball down beyond the goal line of the opposition.

Fullback: The fullback, who is positioned at the back of the pitch, is in charge of fielding high kicks, launching counterattacks, and providing support in both offense and defense.

Dimensions and Markings of a Rugby Field

The limits of play and different zones are delineated by the markings and particular measurements of a rugby field, also known as a pitch.

Rugby fields typically measure around 100 meters (328 feet) in length and 70 meters (229 feet) in width. The in-goal areas, the try line, the touchlines (sidelines), and the midway line are some of the divisions of the field. The goalposts are two uprights with a horizontal crossbar that are placed in the middle of the try line.

Distinct field marks and lines have distinct functions:

The try line designates the spot where players try to plant the ball in order to score a try.

Each try line is 22 meters distant from the 22-Meter Line, which is utilized for lineouts and dropouts.

The 10-Meter Line is used for kickoffs and restarts. It is drawn 10 meters away from the midway line.

Goal Line: In order to score a try, players must cross the goal line, which spans the entire field.

Halfway Line: Used for kickoffs and restarts, this line divides the field into two halves.

RUGBY BALL AND SAFETY EQUIPMENT

Rugby balls have an unusual oval form that makes it easier to hold and pass them. The size and weight of the ball might vary depending on the level of competition, but for international matches, the conventional measurements are a circumference of roughly 28-30 cm (11-12 inches) and a length of 28-31 cm (11-12 inches). Though synthetic materials may be used in more recent models, the ball is typically made of leather.

Rugby players wear specialized protective gear to secure their safety during the physically demanding parts of the game. Rugby is known for having less protective equipment than other contact sports, although players nonetheless don the following:

A mouthguard is an essential piece of safety equipment that guards against concussions and tooth damage.

Some athletes, notably forwards, use scrum caps to protect their heads during scrums and rucks.

Shoulder pads are optional but frequently used by athletes as additional impact protection.

Rugby Boots: To increase traction on the pitch, players don specialist rugby boots with cleats.

Body Padding: Some athletes decide to wear thin padding to safeguard delicate parts like the sternum and ribs.

Try, Conversion, and Penalty Scoring

There are various ways to score in rugby, each of which has its own complexities:

Tries: When a player successfully places the ball in the opponent's in-goal area, a try is scored. It is the main way to score in rugby and is worth five points.

Conversions: After a team scores a try, they are given the chance to try a conversion kick. A conversion kick must travel through the goalposts and be launched from a location perpendicular to the spot where the try was scored. A successful conversion results in an extra two points for the side.

Teams can gain points by successfully kicking penalty goals, which are another type of goal. This is given when the opponent violates a particular rule. From the spot of the infraction, the team may elect to attempt a goal kick; a successful penalty goal is worth three points.

Replacements and Switches

Rugby permits substitutions and interchanges, which have a tactical purpose in controlling player fatigue and adjusting to various game stages.

Rugby teams have the option to completely replace players. As the game develops, substitutions may be made to accommodate injured players, tactical adjustments, or the addition of fresh legs. Once a player has been replaced, they are unable to rejoin the game.

Interchanges are permitted in several forms of rugby, including Rugby League. This implies that players may enter and exit the game repeatedly, frequently during breaks in play.

The amount of interchanges and substitutes that can be made vary depending on the type of rugby being played. For instance, fewer substitutions are permitted in rugby union than rugby league, which allows for more interchanges.

In conclusion, both players and fans must have a thorough understanding of the fundamentals and equipment of rugby. A deeper understanding of the dynamics of the sport results from familiarity with player positions and roles, field dimensions and markings, the special rugby ball and protective gear, the try, conversion, and penalty scoring system, as well as the idea of substitutions and interchanges. Rugby continues to be a game that captivates both players and spectators with its unique blend of intensity, strategy, and camaraderie.

CHAPTER THREE

PASSING AND HANDLING SKILLS IN RUGBY

Rugby players must possess the passing and handling skills necessary to move the ball efficiently and create scoring opportunities. The intricacies of passing and handling skills are covered in depth in this section, including fundamental principles, accurate passing form and technique, unloading and fending, catching high and low balls, evasive running, and changing directions.

Simple Handling Methods

Rugby players must be able to handle the ball with assurance and security. Passing and carrying the ball are built on fundamental handling skills:

Grip: Place both hands on the ball, evenly distributing your fingers over its surface. To provide for control and flexibility, the grip should be firm but not too tight.

Position the ball close to your chest in order to pass it effectively. Keep your body calm and your elbows tucked in.

Maintaining a comfortable finger spread on the ball can help you hold it more securely and handle it better. Fingers should apply light pressure on the ball to keep it steady as it moves.

Vision: While handling the ball, keep your eyes on the targeted objective. You can be aware of your surroundings and potential defenses thanks to peripheral vision.

Accuracy and Proper Passing Form

Rugby collaboration is based on effective passing, which makes it possible to transmit the ball fast and precisely to teammates. In order to pass properly, you must:

Stand with your back to the target and your hips and shoulders straight. Put equal amounts of weight on both feet.

The passing arm should be your dominant hand. To release the ball, snap the handle forward after a backward swing to produce power.

Passing Motion: Flick your wrist as you throw the ball to increase spin and improve accuracy. Instead of your palm, the pass should be released from your fingertips.

Follow Through: Permit your passing hand to continue in the pass's intended direction. This movement improves accuracy and makes sure the pass gets to the desired recipient.

Accuracy over Distance: To ensure accurate delivery on longer passes, concentrate on keeping a firm body position and developing power from your hips and legs.

Fending and Offloading

Techniques for fending and offloading are essential for holding onto the ball and generating attacking opportunities:

Offloading: Before or during a tackle, the ball is sent to a teammate. To catch defenses off surprise and keep the attack moving forward, timing is crucial.

Fending: Also referred to as a "hand-off," fending is employed to ward off defenders. To put some space between you and the tackler, extend your arm and hand. Successful fending depends on timing and body posture.

Chasing Low and High Balls

Keeping possession requires being able to catch both high and low balls, notably on kicks and restarts:

Catching high balls requires you to pay close attention to both the ball's trajectory and its shadow as it falls to the earth. To make a secure catch, place yourself below the ball and utilize your hands. Knees should be slightly bent to reduce landing impact.

Low-bouncing balls should be approached with a low body stance to keep you balanced and prepared to rapidly grab the ball. Scoop the ball with your hands and move it toward your chest.

Evasive Running and Directional Changing

Agile movement and evasive running are essential for outwitting opponents and gaining ground:

Evasive Running: To trick defenders and open doors, use sidesteps, swerves, and variations in speed. To stay balanced and increase your ability to change directions, keep your body low.

Swiftly changing directions enables you to avoid tackles and maintain your evasiveness. Put one foot down firmly and push off in the direction you want to go, using the momentum of your body to carry out the direction change effortlessly.

Finally, the foundation of rugby is passing and handling skills, which allow players to move the ball efficiently, outwit opponents, and create scoring opportunities. Players contribute to the overall strategy and success of their team by acquiring fundamental handling methods, good passing form, and accuracy. The impact of a player on the game is further increased by their ability to unload and evade defenders. For the purpose of keeping possession across various game circumstances, catching high and low balls is crucial. Finally, athletes can get around defenders and gain significant yardage by combining evasive running with direction changes. These abilities together make up the core of rugby's dynamic gameplay, demonstrating the sport's complex fusion of physical prowess and tactical expertise.

CHAPTER FOUR

RUGBY TACKLES AND DEFENSE

Rugby's crucial features of defense and tackling influence games' results and promote team success. In-depth discussions of tackling techniques, defensive line formation, rucking and counter-rucking, defensive tactics for mauls and lineouts, and the skill of tracking and covering opponents are provided in this section.

Low- and High-Intensity Tackling

The essential ability of tackling calls for accuracy, timing, and technique. Different tackling methods are required for various situations:

Low Tackle: A low tackle is when you try to slam into your opponent's legs or hips, usually below the waist. This method works well for taking down an opponent and stopping them from moving forward. Bend your knees, force your shoulder into the opponent's hips, and wrap your arms around their legs to execute a low tackle.

High Tackle: A high tackle primarily focuses above the waist and targets the upper body. High tackles are occasionally required to stop the momentum of a quick opponent, even if they can result in penalties if not executed properly. Aim to wrap your arms around the opponent's chest and shoulders while retaining control and reducing the possibility of risky play when making a high tackle.

Defensive line alignment and formation

To stop opponents from moving through openings, a defensive line that is well-organized is essential. Communication and proper alignment are essential:

Line Speed: A defensive line that functions as a unit moves forward quickly to apply pressure to the opposing team and limit their choices. Attackers are prevented from using gaps by maintaining line speed.

Players should be evenly spaced apart and horizontally oriented throughout the field. This makes sure there are no openings for the assaulting team to take advantage of.

Effective defense line communication aids in identifying threats and signaling defensive line movements.

RUCKING AND COUNTER-RUCKING

Following a tackle, players engage in rucking, a competition for the ball on the ground. Regaining possession or reducing the attacking team's ball recycling are the goals of defensive rucking:

Defensive players must join the ruck from behind the offside line in order to legally confront opponents. This may entail tackling the ball with your hands or pushing opponents away from it.

Counter-Rucking: This strategy interferes with the attacking team's ability to hold onto the ball. Aiming to either win the ball or create a chaotic environment that slows down the attack, defenders aggressively contest the ball.

Lineouts and Mauls: Defensive Techniques

Set pieces like mauls and lineouts require careful consideration of defensive tactics:

Mauls are created when a player carrying the ball is tackled by one or more opponents and one or more of their teammates tie onto them. Defenders can try to halt the maul by lawfully interfering with the ball carrier's movement.

In a lineout, the team receiving the throw-in is required to elevate one of its players in order to collect the ball. In order to defend a lineout, one must interfere with the throw, compete for the ball, and keep the assaulting team from establishing a strong base for their subsequent move.

Following and protecting adversaries

To stop opponents from cutting through the defensive line and gaining territory, it's critical to track and cover them:

Tracking: Defenders need to keep tabs on how attacking players are moving so they can predict their routes. Defenders can limit attacking options and steer opponents toward less advantageous parts of the field by shifting laterally and keeping appropriate spacing.

Covering entails positioning a second defender to stand in for the tackler. If the ball is freed after the tackle, it will be easier to quickly contest for it. Effective covering keeps adversaries from taking advantage of openings left by the first tackler.

In conclusion, the two pillars of effective rugby gameplay are tackling and defense. It's essential to master tackling methods, especially low and high tackles, to stop opponents' advancement and retake possession. A defensive line that is properly aligned, moves quickly, and communicates effectively forms a strong barrier for attackers. In order to contest possession and impede the attacking team's ball recycling, rucking and counter-rucking are essential.

Mauls and lineouts are examples of set pieces that involve strategic awareness and the capacity to thwart the opposition's preparations. Finally, tracking and covering opponents requires being aware of their movements, keeping adequate distance, and being ready to offer assistance when required. Defenders demonstrate the sport's blend of physicality, strategy, and collaboration by mastering these talents and making a substantial contribution to the success of their team.

CHAPTER FIVE

KICKING AND GAME MANAGEMENT IN RUGBY

Rugby relies heavily on kicking, which has a significant impact on both offensive and defensive tactics. This section offers a thorough examination of kicking methods, addressing various methods such the punt, grubber, and drop kick. It also explores the tactical elements of kicking for territory and calculated kicks for goals. The art of goal kicking, which includes conversions and penalties, is also covered, as well as decision making, which entails deciding when to kick, pass, or run.

Various Kicking Methods: Punt, Grubber, and Drop

Depending on the circumstances of the game, rugby offers a variety of kicking tactics, each with a particular purpose:

Kicking a punt: A punt is a high, arching kick that is used to gain ground. It is frequently used when a team is well inside its own half, with the intention of relieving pressure and forcing the opposition back. The trajectory of the punt kick makes it difficult for the opponent to swiftly retaliate.

The grubber kick rolls along the ground at a low, bouncing angle. It is perfect for utilizing open space behind the defensive line to throw opponents off guard, forcing them to act swiftly to recover the ball.

Drop Kick: To perform a drop kick, release the ball and kick it as it rises to the air. It is frequently utilized for drop goals during open play, penalty goals, and conversions after scoring tries. For effective drop kicks, timing and precision are essential.

Kicking for Territory Tactically

A crucial component of game management is tactical kicking for territory. Punts and grubber kicks can be used effectively to achieve a territorial advantage.

Punting: Punting enables the kicker to shoot the ball high and far down the field when a team is well inside its own half. As a result, the kicking side has more time to adjust its defensive positioning while also forcing the opposition to retreat.

Grubber kicks: These deliberate kicks are used to force opponents back into their half. The attacking team can exert pressure on the defense and push them to turn and chase the ball by taking advantage of openings and bouncing the ball into free space.

Strategic Goal-Scoring Kicks

By applying pressure to the defense of opponents, strategic kicks can be used to create scoring opportunities:

A teammate has the chance to chase and receive the ball in a position that could result in a try when the chip kick is used to slightly elevate the ball above the defensive line.

Cross-Field Kick: By kicking the ball from one side of the field to the other, this kick seeks to change the direction of play. When a team notices an overlap or open space on the opposing side, they use it.

Making Decisions: When to Run, Pass, or Kick

Choosing between kicking, passing, and running is essential for managing the game and taking advantage of the best opportunities:

Players must make a quick assessment of the available space and their defensive positioning. If there is room behind the defense, a well-placed kick can gain significant ground.

Finding gaps, mismatches, and defensive flaws when reading defenders can help guide decisions. Players can determine the best course of action by conducting a fast analysis of the circumstance.

Team Strategy: The overall strategy of the team has an impact on decision-making. Teams may focus on gaining territory, keeping the ball, or taking advantage of scoring opportunities depending on the game strategy.

Goalkicking, Conversions and Penalties

Conversions and penalties are important elements in goal-kicking, which entails converting opportunities into points:

Conversions: The attacking side has the opportunity to score two extra points by successfully kicking the ball through the goalposts after scoring a try. Depending on where the try was scored, the kick's angle will change.

Penalties: Penalties allow teams to attempt a goal kick from the location of the offence on the field. Three points are awarded for penalties when the kick is successful.

In conclusion, game management and kicking are essential elements of rugby strategy that call for a combination of time, talent, and awareness. The punt, grubber, and drop kick, among other kicking maneuvers, provide flexible choices for gaining ground, creating scoring possibilities, and upholding defensive pressure. To manage the field position and set the tempo of the game, tactical kicking is essential.

Assessing space, analyzing defenders, and matching decisions to the team's broader strategy are all necessary components of effective decision-making. A skill that can turn potential points into reality is goal kicking, which includes conversions and penalties. These components show how well players and teams can manage the pace of the match, adjust to changing conditions, and ultimately succeed on the rugby field.

CHAPTER SIX

RUGBY TEAM TACTICS AND PLAYBOOKS

Rugby gaming is based on team plans and the playbook, which direct players' decisions and actions on the field. This section covers set plays, like as scrums, lineouts, and kickoffs, and digs deeply into the fine aspects of team plans. The art of adjusting to shifting game circumstances is also covered, along with offensive patterns and movements, exploiting defensive gaps, defending techniques and line speed.

Set Plays: Kickoff, Lineout, and Scrum

Set plays are predetermined moves during particular game scenarios that offer a methodical way to acquire an edge.

Players from each team band together to compete for possession of the ball in a scrum. The scrum is used in set plays that involve strategies to either gain possession and advance or set up an attack.

Players raise a teammate to catch the ball during a lineout, which is tossed in from the touchline. Here, the lifting and timing must be coordinated to ensure a clean catch and a quick change to an attacking rhythm.

Kickoff: Kickoffs are opportunities to take possession and territory that mark the beginning of each half. Specific kickoff trajectories and player placement during set plays can be used to dispute the ball in the air.

Attacking Movements and Patterns

Coordinated actions are used in attacking patterns and moves to create scoring opportunities:

Phase Play: A phase play is a series of controlled passes and runs designed to move the ball forward while scouting the defense for holes. To take advantage of gaps, players move the ball quickly and use support play.

Off-the-Ball Movement: Players who are not directly involved in carrying the ball can nevertheless have an impact on the attack by setting up decoy runs, distracting the ball carrier's defenders, and creating space.

Teams create structured maneuvers that include ahead-of-time planned actions and sequences. These maneuvers may involve complex passing schemes, loop plays, and deception to trick defenders.

Finding Defensive Loopholes

Successful teams take advantage of defensive weaknesses and openings:

Players must read the defensive line to locate any holes brought about by misalignment, a fast-moving line, or overcommitment.

Players must make split-second judgments in order to take advantage of spaces. This could entail making timed passes, offloads, or kicks to profit from the defensive mistakes.

Defensive tactics and line speed

Strong defensive tactics are essential for fending off adversarial attacks:

Line Speed: How quickly the defensive line advances is a crucial component of defense. Attackers are under pressure and have less alternatives and time due to aggressive line pace.

Defense: To reduce openings that attackers could exploit, players must maintain a solid defensive form. Players can respond swiftly to threats when they are aligned properly.

Tackling Technique: A successful defense depends on effective tackling. To effectively take down opponents, players must execute both low and high tackles with the appropriate technique.

Changing Game Situations Adaptation

Rugby is a dynamic sport that requires teams to adjust to shifting circumstances:

Real-Time Decision-Making: Players are required to evaluate the changing conditions and make choices that are consistent with the team's strategy and the developing situation.

Game management: The strategy of the team must be managed by the captains and other important decision-makers. They evaluate when to keep the ball in hand, whether to kick for territory, and when to apply defensive pressure.

Coaches tactically employ replacements to reenergize their teams, address injuries, or change their approach depending on the score and the way the game is going.

The playbook and team plans, which include planned plays, offensive patterns, defensive techniques, and the capacity to adjust to changing circumstances, serve as the blueprint for rugby gameplay. Scrums, lineouts, and kickoffs are examples of set plays that let teams take advantage of one another through deliberate actions. Attacking patterns and moves involve planned activities to open scoring chances and take advantage of defensive weaknesses. To stop opponents from advancing, defensive techniques emphasize line speed, shape, and tackling technique.

Making quick decisions, managing the game effectively, and using replacements strategically are all necessary for adapting to changing game scenarios. Teams can demonstrate their ability to execute complicated moves, develop dynamic attacks, and successfully counter their opponents' strategy by mastering these elements. Rugby is a sport that requires both skillful execution and shrewd game management due to the interaction of these factors, which adds to its allure and complexity.

CONCLUSION

Rugby is a team sport that combines physicality, strategy, and cooperation. It is a tapestry made of numerous complex techniques and tactics. Each aspect of rugby's attraction, from the game's history to the subtlety of team tactics, adds to its distinctive weave.

Rugby was first played spontaneously, and since then it has taken on many different forms, including Rugby Union, Rugby League, and Rugby Sevens. These variations showcase how flexible the sport is and how many different ways there are to participate, enjoy, and compete in it.

Rugby is fundamentally a dynamic fusion of talent and strategy, with player roles and positions serving as the cornerstone of gameplay. Together, the forward packs and backlines use maneuvers like scrummaging, lineouts, rucks, and mauls to gain the ball and advance the ball down the field. These methods highlight how important teamwork and thoughtful execution are in rugby.

The fundamentals of passing and handling are essential to rugby. Players are able to move the ball fluidly, carry out calculated kicks, and open up defenses with the use of these skills. Precision kicks, elusive dashes, and accurate passes lay the foundation for thrilling plays and thrilling tactical moves.

Another essential element that exemplifies rugby's physicality and strategy fusion is defense. A defensive fortress built with low and high tackles, defensive line alignments, and rucking is designed to stop opponents in their tracks. This defensive barrier, strengthened by group efforts, exemplifies rugby's focus on cooperation and coordinated movement.

A successful team's game management, a nuanced interplay of judgment and flexibility, establishes the tone. Set plays are used by teams to create opportunities to exert dominance over their opponents during scrums, lineouts, and kickoffs. The attacking patterns, gap-closing tactics, and defensive line pace are all factors in the game's constantly changing rhythm.

Rugby's capacity to adjust to shifting game scenarios lies at the center of this ballet of tactics and abilities. Rugby exhibits a fluidity that keeps players and viewers alike on the edge of their seats, whether it is through quick decisions made on the field, tactical tweaks, or well-timed substitutions.

In conclusion, rugby's multidimensional gameplay encompasses an entire universe of complexity. Rugby's history is one of evolution and growth, from the first playing fields to the contemporary stadiums that stage world championships. A sport that combines physical prowess, strategic thinking, and teamwork results in a captivating spectacle and a real test of character. Players contribute to rugby's ever-evolving history by executing intricate passes, making hard tackles, and planning tactical masterstrokes. Rugby's legacy is defined by the symphony of abilities and strategies that make this sport an enduring and enthralling spectacle for everyone who participates in it.

THANK YOU

Printed in Great Britain
by Amazon